WATCY

We hope you enjoy this book.
Please return or renew it by the due date.
You can renew it at **www.norfolk.gov.uk/libraries**
or by using our free library app. Otherwise you can
phone **0344 800 8020** - please have your library
card and pin ready.
You can sign up for email reminders too.

NORFOLK COUNTY COUNCIL
LIBRARY AND INFORMATION SERVICE

NORFOLK ITEM

3 0129 08398 9971

OXFORD
UNIVERSITY PRESS

Great Clarendon Street, Oxford, OX2 6DP,
United Kingdom

Oxford University Press is a department of the University of Oxford.
It furthers the University's objective of excellence in research, scholarship,
and education by publishing worldwide. Oxford is a registered trade mark of
Oxford University Press in the UK and in certain other countries

Text © Dan Metcalf 2017

Illustrations © Robin Boyden 2017

The moral rights of the author have been asserted

First published 2017

British Library Cataloguing in Publication Data
Data available

978-0-19-837762-7

5 7 9 10 8 6 4

Paper used in the production of this book is a natural, recyclable product
made from wood grown in sustainable forests. The manufacturing process
conforms to the environmental regulations of the country of origin.

Printed in China by Golden Cup

Acknowledgements
Inside cover notes written by Gill Howell

For Chunky x

Contents

Chapter 1
Slug Magnet

"Aaargh! I've found another one!" shouted Jamie, holding a slimy, squishy slug between his thumb and his fingers. "They're everywhere!"

On the other side of the garden, Jamie's sister Daisy laughed.

"They must like you, Jamie! You're a slug magnet!"

Jamie made a face at his sister and turned back to his vegetable patch. They were at their grandad's house, where they were helping him with his gardening.

Grandad Jim had a beautiful garden, full of flowers and shrubs. He had made two square vegetable patches for Jamie and Daisy to look after. Daisy's patch was amazing. It had large bunches of carrots, huge pumpkins, tall sticks of runner beans and bright red tomatoes. Jamie's, however, was weedy, dead and full of slugs. His lettuce had more holes than his socks, and his herbs were as

limp and puny as a wet flannel. Jamie
looked over at Daisy's patch.

"What can I say, Jamie?" said Daisy.
"Some of us have green fingers, and
some of us don't!"

"Stupid slugs!" Jamie muttered,
turning back to his patch of earth.
"Eating all my veggies! I bet you
wouldn't dare come near my patch if I
had my micro-blaster ray!"

Jamie had a secret. He wasn't just a schoolboy, little brother and slug magnet. He was a Galaxy Defender!

Just six months ago, the president of the entire galaxy had sent out a mind-scan across the planets. He was searching for the most brilliant heroes in the galaxy. Their job would be to travel through space, stopping crime and fighting evil. No one was more surprised than Jamie when the mind-scan found that he was the best person on planet Earth to do the job! It didn't matter that he was only eight years old, the president had said. All the best Galaxy Defenders were.

While he was on Earth, Jamie had to keep his special job top secret but whenever he got an emergency call, he had to dash off and save the galaxy. It was tricky balancing his normal life with his secret space life, but it was such an exciting job that he never complained. He had his own rocket ship, a robot crewmate and lots of gadgets to help him in his quests.

Today though, he had a muddy trowel and some revolting slugs to deal with. He picked one up and cheekily threw it on to Daisy's patch.

"Hey!" she screamed. "Grandad! Jamie's throwing slugs!"

"The slug likes Daisy!" smiled Jamie. "He said he wanted to kiss her!"

Grandad Jim came out of his shed. "Pack it in, both of you," he said. "Or I'll get my friend to deal with you!"

He pointed to a life-sized model of a policeman. It wore an old blue suit and had a sack for a head, with one of Jamie's old dressing-up police helmets on the top.

"What in the galaxy is that?" asked Jamie.

"This is my new scarecrow!" said Grandad Jim. "He's going to stop the birds coming down and pecking at my new seeds. When they see him standing here, they'll think he's real and fly away."

Grandad stuck the policeman into the ground with a long pole. He took a step back to look at it and a large blackbird flew down on to the scarecrow's shoulder.

"Aaargh! Get away! Shoo!" shouted Grandad, running at the bird and waving his arms like a windmill. Jamie and Daisy laughed.

"I think your scarecrow needs to be a bit scarier, Grandad!" said Jamie.

"Yeah, you should stick Jamie there. He'd scare anything away, except the slugs!" said Daisy.

"Hey!" said Jamie.

"Ha! You're just jealous that my veggie patch is blooming!"

"Blooming horrible, more like!" sulked Jamie. He looked over at Daisy's vegetables and then back over to his own. She was right. His plants were tiny compared to her monsters. He would love to show her a thing or two and have the prize-winning veggies at the village fair.

Just then, Jamie's watch started to flash and buzz. He hid it quickly behind his back. It was his special Galacto-Watch. Someone, somewhere, was in trouble and needed his help! He dropped his trowel.

"I, er, need to go back home and get something," he said.

Jamie only lived a few doors away, so Grandad walked him to the gate and watched him hurry down the pavement.

"Stay safe, Jamie!" he called.

"I'll try!" he called back. "Right then," he muttered to himself as he opened his front door. "Let's go and save the galaxy!"

Chapter 2
The Mission

Jamie dashed past his mum and dad, who were in the lounge reading their books. Dad was reading a book on stargazing. He loved anything to do with space and Jamie really wanted to tell him his secret, but he wasn't allowed. It was a shame, thought Jamie. Dad would love to see the galaxy from Jamie's rocket instead of looking at it through a telescope!

Mum looked up. "Hello, Jamie! Wash your hands if you've been gardening!"

Jamie quickly washed his hands and ran into his room. He pressed his Galacto-Watch against the wardrobe door. The door beeped and Jamie opened it up.

Inside the wardrobe was a big screen with lights and dials on it. This was the Super Link screen that allowed him to talk to the rest of the galaxy, and it only

appeared for him. (Whenever Mum or Dad came to open the wardrobe, all they found were a few school jumpers and jeans.) The screen fizzed and crackled, then cleared to show a smiling, thin man with an orange face and two purple ears on top of his head.

"Ah, Defender Jones! I'm so glad you could call. Let me show you something!"

President Zink was the man in charge of the whole galaxy! He bent down and reappeared holding a kitten with black and white stripes, and huge fangs. "Let me introduce you to Tiddlez. Isn't she cute?" Tiddlez looked like a miniature tiger and was playfully trying to bite President Zink's ears off. "We got her to chase the mice at the Galactic Palace. The only problem is that the mice are bigger than her! Still, she loves to play and give me cuddles, don't you girl?" Zink tickled the beast under her chin and the kitten purred happily.

"Um … sir? The emergency?" said Jamie.

"Hmm? Ah, yes! Jones, take your rocket to Lubon 3. It's a farming planet in sector 7G. They're having problems with the harvest and need your help urgently."

"Yes, sir! Right away!" Jamie said, saluting.

"Very good. Stay on the line and Quirby will brief you about the gadgets you may need. Zink over and out."

The screen crackled again and President Zink was replaced by a large, happy-looking blue alien with glasses and a white lab coat.

"Hello, Quirby!" called Jamie. He liked to see his friend. Quirby always had a cool gadget to give him. Sometimes the gadgets would save Jamie's life!

"'Ello Jamie! Are you OK? You look a bit pink!"

"That's my normal colour, Quirby!" laughed Jamie. "You look a bit blue to me! What have you got?"

Quirby pulled out something that looked like a cross between a complicated phone and a small walkie-talkie.

"This is *sooo* cool! It's a 3D Holophone! It projects a hologram of the person you are calling," she said. "And this is a high-frequency radio, for when your rocket's Super Link is out of range."

She flicked a switch on the radio and a high-pitched squeal sounded. She quickly shut it off. "I'm sure you'll work out how to use it. I'm beaming them over now. Good luck! Quirby over and out."

The 3D phone and radio materialized in a second at the bottom of the wardrobe. Jamie grabbed them and pressed a button on the Super Link screen. With a whir and a clunk, the wardrobe spun around. Suddenly, Jamie was standing in his rocket ship, which was hidden inside his bedroom's chimney. He quickly climbed into his red jumpsuit and put on his helmet.

"Hello, Jamie. Setting co-ordinates for Lubon 3," said a voice. It was Buzz, his robotic co-pilot. Buzz lived on the rocket, making sure it was always in tip-top condition. Jamie was always impressed at how clean and tidy Buzz kept it, especially as he was no bigger than a bumblebee.

"Thanks, Buzz," said Jamie. "Start the countdown, please. Let's go and help this planet." Jamie sat down in the cockpit and felt the engines hum underneath him.

"Lift-off in three …"

Jamie fastened his seatbelt.

"Two …"

The rocket shook …

"One … Blast off!"

"Here we go!" yelled Jamie over the roar of the engines.

KA-FROOM!

The rocket blasted off at light speed. It was so quick that no one noticed the red rocket zooming out of Jamie's house. In space, the stars whipped past them and in a matter of seconds, they were entering the atmosphere of Lubon 3.

"Jamie, look out! Incoming attack!" Buzz shouted.

"Huh?" Jamie looked out of the window to see Lubon 3 rushing towards them. As the rocket was about to come in to land, Jamie could just make out a figure ahead of them. It was a man in a black cape and hat, holding a large energy blaster. The man grinned and started zapping energy beams directly at the rocket!

Chapter 3
Crash Landing

THRWOOM!

Jamie managed to swerve the rocket out of the way and avoid a nasty crash. He wasn't so lucky when the second energy beam came at him, flashing past the window and clipping a tail fin. It sent Jamie spinning out of control, whizzing through the air! He held on tight and there was a huge CRASH!

He looked around seconds later to find himself upside down, held tight in his seat by his safety belt.

"Are you OK, Jamie?" said Buzz.

"I'm fine, Buzz," Jamie answered. "I don't think the rocket is, though. Can you run some tests?"

Jamie unbuckled his seat belt and fell to the floor (which, as the rocket was upside down, was the ceiling).

"A tail fin is damaged, Jamie. It'll take me and the Insectibots five point three hours to fix it."

"That's great, Buzz. That gives me just enough time to find the locals and fix their problem," said Jamie, as he put on his special spacesuit.

Buzz released his army of Insectibots – tiny robots that flew around in a swarm like flies and could fix anything by working together.

Jamie stepped out of the rocket and on to the muddy ground of Lubon 3. He had crash-landed in a field with rows and rows of vegetables underneath a beautiful purple sky.

He looked around and spotted a small village at the end of the field. Jamie thought that the village was made of thatched huts but as he got closer, he could see that they were in fact giant mushrooms which had been hollowed out with a door fixed to the front.

He trudged through the mud until he came to the edge of the village.

"HALT! Who goes there?" said a voice from the shadows. "Friend or foe?"

Jamie raised his hands.

"Friend!" he said. "Jamie Jones, Galaxy Defender. I'm responding to a distress call from the local tribe."

Slowly, a figure came out of the shadows. The alien was young and carried a bottle, her finger on the spray trigger.

"But you're just a boy!" said the alien, disappointed.

"And you're just a … just a …" Jamie struggled for a word. He had seen many strange creatures in his travels of the galaxy, but never one like this. The alien looked like a giant leek! She had white feet, a green head and was tall and thin.

"We are the Lubobo. We farm the land here on Lubon 3. You can call me Lyka."

She lowered the bottle, which Jamie now saw said 'Weedkiller' on the side. "Are you … *vegetables?*" he asked, finally. Lyka walked back to a small mushroom hut and Jamie followed.

"I suppose we are, yes. There are many vegetable life forms in this part of the galaxy." They entered the mushroom hut. There was a small fire for warmth, a large window to let in the sun, and some stools. Lyka offered Jamie a seat.

31

"Soil? Freshly dug today!"

"Er … thanks," said Jamie, confused.

Lyka gave him a bucket full of
sludgy soil and sat down with one for
herself. For a moment Jamie thought
he was expected to drink it, but then he
saw Lyka sink her feet into the brown
mixture.

"Of course!" thought Jamie.
"Vegetables take in food through their
roots from soil. This bucket of sludge is
like being offered a cup of tea and a slice
of cake!"

He didn't want to upset Lyka, so he stuck his boots into the mud.

"Mmm, lovely!" he smiled. "How can I help?"

Lyka explained that her people worked on the fields, producing fruit and vegetables for the whole galaxy, but recently one of their crops had been taken.

"The man who fired at you with the energy blaster was The Crow. He is a poacher, travelling from planet to planet, stealing crops from the ground."

Jamie sighed. Was this why he had been brought millions of miles through space? To stop someone stealing a few space-cucumbers? Lyka saw the disappointed look on his face.

"I don't think you realize!" she said angrily. "This man is putting my people in danger! He comes here and steals the Seedlings."

"But you must have lots of seeds. Can't you just grow some more?" said Jamie.

"We can't – the Seedlings aren't like normal crops. They are the seeds of the Lubobo!" said Lyka.

Jamie gasped. The Lubobo must have grown from the ground like all other plants. If The Crow was stealing seeds, that meant he was stealing their children!

Jamie stood, squelching in his bucket of mud. "There's no time to lose!" he said.

"You will help us?" said Lyka.

Jamie placed a hand on her shoulder.

"I'll catch The Crow and bring him to justice. You can rely on me!"

Jamie clumsily shook the mud off his feet and marched out of the village with Lyka, back towards the crashed rocket. As he left, crowds of Lubobo clapped their leafy green hands together, cheering him on.

Chapter 4
Hatching a Plan

When Jamie and Lyka got back to the rocket, Buzz and the Insectibots were doing a good job of fixing it, but it wasn't ready yet. Jamie decided to check his supplies, laying them out on the ground.

"Let's see," he pondered. "We've got a Holophone, hundreds of metres of spare electrical wire, a blaster ray and my Porta-Cell."

Jamie showed the Porta-Cell to Lyka. It looked like a rolled-up rubber mat, but when he laid it on the ground and tapped his Galacto-Watch, golden laser beams fired upwards, making the bars of a jail cell. With this little gadget, he could contain any villain in the universe once they were caught.

"What does this do?" said Lyka. She hit a button on the high-frequency radio

Quirby had given Jamie and a deafening
shriek came from it. Lyka dropped it,
putting her hands up to her ears. (Until
just now, Jamie hadn't even been sure
where her ears were.) Jamie quickly shut
the radio off.

"I'm not quite sure *what* it does, to be honest!" he laughed. An idea hit him. "That's it! We'll set up a trap!" He grabbed his supplies and they walked over to a plot, where he explained his plan to Lyka.

He would make a small tripwire around the edge of the plot and attach the end to the radio. "When The Crow returns, he'll trip on the wire, which will turn on the radio. That horrible noise will blast out and stop him for long enough for me to put him in my Porta-Cell!"

"I hope it works!" said Lyka. She took a bottle from her belt and sipped from it.

"What's that?" asked Jamie. "I thought vegetables only took in food from the soil?"

"We walking, talking veggies need something a bit more powerful!" Lyka smiled. "I always carry a bottle of cosmic compost juice. It keeps my leaves green and my roots nice and long! Would you like to try some? It's made from the dung of the giant moon-cows of Dobo 8."

Jamie politely refused and got back to work.

Jamie and Lyka worked hard setting the trap. They stretched the wires out tight, making a small fence around the plot. Then they attached one end to the radio and sat back. They didn't have to wait for long, as The Crow soon came walking over a nearby field. Jamie and Lyka ducked behind a tree stump to see if their plan would work.

"This way!" whispered Jamie. He held his breath as The Crow stepped down from his spaceship and slung a sack over his shoulder. His black cape flew behind him as he walked towards the plot, and Jamie heard his deep, rumbling laugh. The plot was full of Lubobo Seedlings – he was going to steal more leek babies!

"Wait until I get my hands on him!" said Lyka. "I'm going to make a soup out of him!"

They leaned forward to get a closer look at their trap. The Crow was almost at the plot and hadn't seen the tripwire.

"Here we go!" said Jamie.

The Crow stepped into the plot, his foot hitting the wire …

TWANG!

The wire pinged, setting off the radio. Jamie and Lyka braced themselves for a high-pitched din, but instead were met with a strange sound:

SHOOWOP-A-BEE-BOP-A-LOO-BEE-DO-WAH!

The field and hills around them were filled with the sound of rock-n-roll! The radio must have switched channels when they set the trap, and was now playing music from an intergalactic radio station!

"Oh no! That's not going to frighten him away!" said Jamie, but it was worse than they thought. The Crow looked up, confused.

"Uh-oh," said Lyka. "I think he's heard us!"

Jamie saw that the villain had turned towards them. He was furious, snarling and cawing.

His eyes glowed red as he stared around the field, finally spotting Jamie. He growled in anger. He started to stride across the muddy ground, jolly rock-n-roll music still playing in the background.

"Double uh-oh!" said Lyka. "He's heading straight for us!"

Jamie gulped as The Crow grinned, showing a row of yellow teeth. He reached for his energy blaster.

"Quick, Jamie!" said Lyka, panicking. "What are we going to do?"

Jamie gulped.

"It's OK, that energy blaster only fires energy balls. Enough to knock us down but nothing more. Maybe I can talk to him and … "

BLAM!

The Crow fired his energy blaster, sending a yellow beam through the air. The bolt of energy landed a short distance from Jamie and Lyka, sending mud flying.

"Aagh!" screamed Lyka. "What's the plan, Jamie?"

"Run for it!"

Chapter 5
Plan B

Jamie and Lyka ran away from The Crow, squelching through the wet mud of the fields and ducking for cover.

BOOM!

The energy blaster fired again: the beam flashed past Jamie, hitting a nearby tree.

"Great plan!" shouted Lyka, breathless. "Got any others?"

Jamie reached down to find the Holophone that Quirby had given him. He was scared and really wanted to call his Grandad Jim to save him, but he couldn't. He'd have given anything to be back in the garden, helping out with the weeding. Just then, a picture of his grandad's garden came into his head and an idea struck!

"That's it!" he yelled. "Lyka, I need you to run the other way and make

him chase you while I set up my plan.
Please?"

"WHAT?" Lyka cried. She sighed.
"This had better be a *really* good plan!"
she said. She sped off into a field of
corn, disappearing into the tall rows.
"Oi, bird brain! Over here!" she yelled.

Jamie hid behind a tree and watched as The Crow listened for Lyka's voice and ran after her. Jamie quickly tapped his Holophone and dialled. After a second, he got an answer.

"Jones! How's the mission going?" said President Zink, appearing in front of Jamie as a life-size hologram.

"Um … not quite how I planned, sir," admitted Jamie. "I need you to put Tiddlez on the phone." The president laughed.

"Tiddlez? She's just a kitten!"

"Please, just point the Holophone at her!"

The president turned the phone around and a hologram of the vicious-looking kitten popped up in front of Jamie. The image was clear and very lifelike. Jamie fiddled with the phone handset and found a button marked 'Record'. Tiddlez let out a small 'meow', showing her sharp, tiny fangs.

"That's great, President Zink. Thank you!"

Jamie dashed over to the field of corn, where Lyka was still being chased by The Crow.

"You took your time!" she yelled, running past him.

"All part of the plan!" Jamie said. He fiddled with the Holophone and hit the 'Play' button. The image of Tiddlez meowing was projected into mid-air. At the end of the row of corn, The Crow appeared, grinning menacingly.

"This is no time to be showing him your pets!" said Lyka.

Jamie concentrated and found the button marked 'Enlarge'. He hit it and the hologram of Tiddlez grew until she was the size of a giant tiger! The Crow froze, frightened by the huge moggy in front of him. The clip of Tiddlez meowing and licking her lips played again and again. The sound had been made louder too, so it sounded like the kitten was letting out a giant ROAR!

The villain dropped his energy blaster and fled, running back towards his spaceship. Jamie chased after him.

"Keep running, birdy!" he said. "Just a bit further!"

The Crow ran in fear from the giant kitten, too scared to look where he was going. He stepped on to the rubber mat of Jamie's Porta-Cell and Jamie hit his Galacto-Watch. Golden laser beams shot

up, trapping The Crow.

"GRRRAAAAGGHHH!" cried
The Crow.

"You did it! You really did it!" said
Lyka, jumping up and down with joy.
"Will he go to jail now?"

"Yep," said Jamie, catching his breath.
"He'll be going away for a long time.
If he's lucky, he might get a job in the
prison vegetable plots!"

***

Jamie stood by his rocket, watching a robotic arm lift the Porta-Cell into the cargo bay. The Crow stood inside, looking glum and quiet.

"Jamie, where did you get the idea to project a hologram?" said Lyka. She stood with her family and friends. They were all relieved that The Crow would be going away for good this time.

"Oh, I just remembered something from home," said Jamie. "My grandad uses a scarecrow to keep crows off his garden. I realized we needed a scarecrow of our own, and what could be scarier than a great big kitten with claws and fangs?" He laughed. "I guess this is goodbye, Lyka."

"Thank you, Jamie Jones!" said Lyka. She handed him a small wrapped present. "A gift, to show our thanks."

Jamie unwrapped it and smiled. "Cosmic compost juice! You shouldn't

have!" he said. He sniffed the bottle.
"Ugh, she really shouldn't have!"
he thought.

Lyka gave him a hug and he climbed
on to the rocket. The engines roared and
it zoomed up into the sky. Jamie waved
at the crowd of cheering veggie-aliens
from the cockpit.

Chapter 6
Homeward Bound

Jamie brought the rocket down inside its secret base in the chimney, arriving back at home just a few moments after he had left. That was the beauty of intergalactic travel at speeds faster than light – he could fly across the galaxy, save a planet from thieves or destruction, and be back in time for tea. His mum and dad didn't even notice he had gone! Back in his bedroom, he slipped out of his jumpsuit and into his normal jeans and T-shirt.

He opened the wardrobe and tapped his Super Link screen. President Zink popped up on the monitor.

"Hello, Jones! I trust all went well?"

"Yes, sir," said Jamie. "I dropped The Crow off at Galaxy Defender Headquarters. He should be on his way to prison by now."

"Yes, we'll make sure he doesn't bother anyone again. Good job, Defender!" said President Zink with a wink.

"Thank you, sir! And say thank you to Tiddlez."

"I will, Jones, once she's finished mauling the presidential throne. Good work today. Over and out!"

Jamie ran downstairs and went back over to Grandad Jim's house, joined by his mum and dad.

"I hope your grandad hasn't been working you too hard! Let's see how the garden is looking," said Dad. "How are your veggies getting on, Jamie?"

Jamie groaned. "Well, they make great slug food but I wouldn't eat them myself. Daisy's are amazing, though." He sighed. "I'll never get my veggies into the village fair."

"We'll be the judge of that!" Mum laughed, putting her arm around him. "How about Dad and I judge between your patch and Daisy's? Just for fun of course!"

They turned the corner into the garden. Jamie gasped! Stood in the middle of the vegetables was a tall figure in a black cloak and hat!

"The Crow! He's escaped! Everybody get down!" shouted Jamie. He pushed his dad out of the way and leaped on the tall figure, wrestling him to the ground. He fought for a few seconds and ripped off The Crow's hat to reveal … a bag full of straw!

"What are you doing with my scarecrow?" said Grandad Jim.

Jamie looked down. He was sitting on a man made of hay.

"Your *scarecrow*?" he repeated, embarrassed. He climbed off and brushed himself down. He straightened the scarecrow up and blushed. It was clearly made out of an old sack.

"You said I should make it scarier, remember? So I put my old rain cloak and a mask on it."

"It worked!" laughed Daisy. "It scared the pants off Jamie!"

Everyone laughed except Jamie, who felt very silly.

"We're going to judge your veggies, Daisy," said Mum. "Let's see how they're doing." Daisy led Mum over to her patch, sneering at Jamie.

"It's hardly a fair contest," said Daisy. "Jamie's are barely alive! I'll win easily."

Jamie watched as they all spoke about how well Daisy's plants were doing. He sighed and sat down on the grass. If only he could—

He felt something uncomfortable in his back pocket and fished it out.

"Of course!" he said to himself as he saw what it was. "The cosmic compost juice! Just a few drops should do the trick …"

Jamie poured a drop of the juice from the bottle on to his vegetables and stood back.

WOOOOOOOOMPH!

The vegetables grew in front of his very eyes, expanding and bloating up to incredible sizes! His cucumbers suddenly became the length of snooker cues! His runner beans were as long as his arms! And his marrow was the size of a car!

The whole family turned back to inspect Jamie's patch, and their mouths dropped open in shock. Jamie leaned casually on a tomato the size of an armchair.

"But … what did you … HOW?" said Daisy, amazed.

"What can I say, Daisy?" he grinned. "Some of us have green fingers, and some of us don't!"

About the author

I've always loved writing, ever since I was at school. Back then I was just called a daydreamer, but now I'm a *professional* daydreamer. My job is to make things up and write them down.

The story of Jamie Jones came from a lifelong love of science fiction. One day I just thought of the title *Jamie Jones: Galaxy Defender (aged 8 ½)* and the story sprang from there. I thought of all the cool things I would want if I were an eight year old, space-travelling planet protector and what sort of trouble I would get into. I suppose I'm not too far away from being in space myself – I already live with my head in the clouds!